ADVENTURES WITH ATOMS AND MOLECULES
BOOK IV

CHEMISTRY EXPERIMENTS FOR YOUNG PEOPLE

ROBERT C. MEBANE

THOMAS R. RYBOLT

Enslow Publishers, Inc.

44 Fadem Road   PO Box 38
Box 699   Aldershot
Springfield, NJ 07081   Hants GU12 6BP
USA   UK

ACKNOWLEDGMENT

We wish to thank Paula Watson and Ann Rybolt for reviewing the manuscript.

DEDICATION

This book is dedicated to Alexandra Lancaster-King and to Leah, Megan, Ben, and Karen Rybolt.

Library of Congress Cataloging-in-Publication Data

Mebane, Robert C.
    Adventures with atoms and molecules.
    Includes indexes.
    Chemistry experiments for home or school demonstrate the properties and behavior of various kinds of atoms and molecules.
    1. Chemistry—Experiments—Juvenile literature. 2. Chemistry—Experiments. 3. Molecules—Experiments. 4. Experiments. I. Rybolt, Thomas R. II. Title.
    QD38.M43 1985 540'.78 85-10177
    ISBN 0-7660-1224-7 (bk. 1 pbk)
    ISBN 0-7660-1225-5 (bk. 2 pbk)
    ISBN 0-7660-1226-3 (bk. 3 pbk)
    ISBN 0-7660-1227-1 (bk. 4 pbk)

Printed in the United States of America

10 9 8 7 6 5 4 3 2 1

Cover Illustration: © Corel Corporation

CONTENTS

FOREWORD

This is the fourth in a series of books of hands-on chemistry experiments for young people. Continuing in the same format, the authors have written a new set of interesting, "NEAT," "WOW" activities. Can you use an orange peel as an insecticide? Why does the surface of an egg yolk turn green during cooking? Can you freeze water with ice? Each activity concludes with an explanation and ideas for "Other things to try."

The activities in this series are suitable for girls and boys in upper elementary and middle schools. The experiments encourage children to discover and observe the many changes that occur in their world. In addition, these books provide ideas for science fair investigations.

With the publication of Book IV, Mebane and Rybolt have given young people a total of 120 exciting chemistry experiments to investigate. The experiments are designed to be safe and use materials readily found in the home.

The authors, once again, provide a way to encourage young people to study chemistry.

Ronald I. Perkins
Assistant Director
Institute for Chemical Education
University of Wisconsin—Madison

INTRODUCTION

SCIENCE

Science is an adventure! Science is an adventure of asking questions and finding answers. Scientists are men and women who ask questions. Scientists answer questions by doing experiments and making observations. The results of their observations increase our knowledge and improve our understanding of the world around us.

Science is exciting because it never stops. There will always be new questions to ask. New questions lead to new experiments. New experiments lead to new knowledge and to new questions.

Experimentation is the heart of science. Experimentation lays the foundation upon which the basic principles of science are understood. You can gain a better feeling as to what science really is by doing science and experiencing science.

One way to share in the adventure of science is to do experiments. In our first three books, Adventures With Atoms and Molecules, Adventures With Atoms and Molecules, Book II, and Adventures With Atoms and Molecules, Book III, we presented ninety experiments and suggestions for over one-hundred-eighty additional activities. Those books were a start, but there are many more experiments waiting to be done.

This book is a further collection of experiments that you can do at home or at school. These experiments will help you learn how to ask questions and find answers and how to become a better observer. As you read about science and do experiments, you will learn more about yourself and your world. In asking questions and doing experiments, you will learn that observing and trying to understand the world around you is interesting and fun.

ATOMS, IONS, AND MOLECULES

One of the most important things that scientists have learned about our world is that EVERYTHING IS MADE OF ATOMS. Water, ice, air, sand, table salt, sugar, rocks, shoes, clothes, houses, bicycles, cars, leaves, trees, flowers, bees, ants, spiders, cows, horses, and people are all made of atoms.

Atoms are the basic building blocks of all things. There are ninety-two different kinds of natural atoms. A few additional atoms have been made by scientists in laboratories. Examples of natural atoms include: oxygen, hydrogen, carbon, mercury, gold, silver, helium, chlorine, neon, nickel, iron, phosphorus, and aluminum.

Atoms are found in all things. For example, a piece of aluminum foil is made of aluminum atoms. A diamond consists of carbon atoms. Sand is made of silicon and oxygen atoms. Table sugar is made of carbon, hydrogen, and oxygen atoms.

Molecules are combinations of tightly bound atoms. Water is a combination of hydrogen and oxygen atoms. Imagine you have a drop of water and you divide this drop into smaller and smaller drops. If you could continue to divide the drops enough times, you would eventually end up with a single water molecule. If you divided this water molecule any further, you would have two hydrogen atoms and one oxygen atom.

Scientists use models to represent molecules. Sometimes the models are made from small balls with the balls representing atoms. These models allow scientists to understand more about molecules.

Molecules that are made of only a few atoms are very small. Molecules are so small that you cannot see one even with the most powerful optical microscope. One drop of water contains about two million quadrillion (2,000,000,000,000,000,000,000) molecules. If you took two million quadrillion pennies and stacked one on top of the other, you could make three hundred thousand (300,000) stacks of pennies. Each stack would reach from the Sun to Pluto. Pluto is the planet in our solar system that is the greatest distance from the sun.

If you could magnify one drop of water to the size of the earth, each water molecule would be about the size of an orange.

Polymers are giant molecules made by combining many smaller molecules. Some polymer molecules may contain several million atoms. Important natural polymers include natural rubber, starch, and DNA. Rubber bands and some automobile tires are made of natural rubber. Starch is found in many foods. DNA is the molecule of heredity. Some important polymers made by scientists are nylon, which is used in making fabrics; polyethylene, which is used in making plastic bags and plastic bottles; and polystyrene, which is used in making styrofoam cups and insulation.

Atoms are made of smaller particles. These smaller particles are electrons, protons, and neutrons. The nucleus is the center of the atom and contains protons and neutrons. Protons are positively charged, and neutrons have no charge. Electrons are negatively charged and are found around the nucleus.

Atoms and molecules that contain a charge are called ions. Ions have either a positive charge or a negative charge. Positive ions have more protons than electrons. Negative ions have more electrons than protons. Sodium chloride, which is the chemical name for table salt, is made of positive sodium ions and negative chlorine ions.

Atoms or ions sometimes combine in chemical reactions to make molecules, metal alloys, or salts. Chemical reactions can also involve changing one molecule into a different molecule or breaking one molecule down into smaller molecules, atoms, or ions.

ABOUT THE EXPERIMENTS IN THIS BOOK

In this book we present thirty experiments and suggestions for more than sixty additional activities. Many of the new experiments will show you how experimentation can be used to understand phenomena you encounter in your everyday life. Have you ever wondered why evaporation causes cooling, why wet sand is firmer than dry sand, why sunsets are red, why an egg becomes firm when cooked, what causes a rainbow, how oil lets you see through paper, or why popcorn pops? You will find out through some of the experiments in this book.

Each experiment is divided into five parts: 1) materials, 2) procedure, 3) observations, 4) discussion, and 5) other things to try. The materials are what you need to do the experiment. The procedure is what you do. The observations are what you see. The discussion explains what your observations tell you about atoms and molecules. The other things to try are additional questions and experiments that you can do to find out more about atoms and molecules.

This book is intended to be used and not just read. It is a guide toward doing, observing, and thinking science. The experimental activities described in this book are designed to give you an opportunity to experience science.

Do not worry about trying to understand everything about an experiment. You do not have to memorize words or meanings when you are first involved in science. You need to experience science first.

You do not have to do the experiments in the order they appear in the book. Each experimental activity has been written to stand completely alone. You will find that some experiments discuss the same ideas. It will help you learn and understand these ideas to see them more than once.

Not every experiment you do will work the way you expect every time. Something may be different in the experiment when you do it. Repeat the experiment if it gives an unexpected result and think about what may be different.

Not all of the experiments in this book give immediate results. Some experiments in this book will take time to see observable results. Some of the experiments in this book may take a shorter time than that suggested in the experiment. Some experiments may take a longer time than suggested. You must be patient when doing experiments.

The drawings in this book were done using a computer graphics system. They are not intended to be a photographic or artistic substitution for what you will do and observe. The purpose of the drawings is to direct your attention to one or two key features of what you may expect to observe when you do each experiment.

SAFETY NOTE

MAKE SURE YOU

1) Obtain an adult's permission before you do these experiments and activities.

2) Get an adult to watch you when you do an experiment. They enjoy seeing experiments too.

3) Follow the specific directions given for each experiment.

4) Clean up after each experiment.

NOTE TO TEACHERS, PARENTS, AND OTHER ADULTS

All of us are born with a natural curiosity regarding the world around us. This intrinsic interest in nature is the motivation for most scientific activity. To avoid a dulling of this interest as children grow older, it is necessary to provide experiences for young people that show the connection of science to everyday life and the world around us.

Science is not merely a collection of facts but a way of thinking. Our series of books—Adventures With Atoms and Molecules—is a tool to help children and young people become actively involved in the process of science. Explanations for each experimental activity are provided for completeness, but the experience of the activity is more important than the explanation. The experience can last a lifetime, and understanding can develop with time.

As teachers, parents, and other adults, you can play a key role in maintaining and encouraging a young person's interest in science. As you do experiments with a young person, you may find your own curiosity being expanded.

Remember, science is for everyone!

The adventure continues . . .

DO BUBBLES FORM IN A GLASS OF COLD WATER WHEN THE WATER BECOMES WARM?

Materials

A tall, clear glass   Cold water from sink faucet

Procedure

This experiment works best in the winter when water from a sink faucet is usually colder. If the experiment does not work as expected with cold water from your sink faucet, try the second experiment described in "Other things to try."

Fill a tall, clear glass almost full with cold water from a sink faucet. Put the glass of water in a warm place where it will not be disturbed. A window that gets plenty of sunshine is a good place. Look at the glass of water after five minutes.

Look at the glass after it has sat several hours in a warm spot.

Observations

Do you see any bubbles sticking to the inside of the glass after it has sat in a warm place for five minutes? Do you see any bubbles sticking to the inside of the glass after it has sat in a warm place for several hours?

Discussion

Air is a gas that can dissolve in water. When air dissolves in water, individual molecules in the air become surrounded by water molecules. The molecules in the air are very weakly attracted by water molecules. This weak attraction of molecules in the air and water molecules is what causes some air to dissolve in water.

More molecules in the air will dissolve in cold water than in hot water. Water and molecules in the air move slower when they are cold.

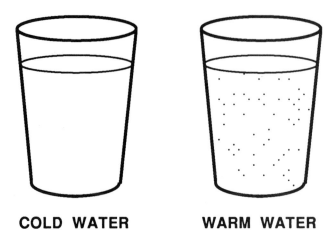

COLD WATER   **WARM WATER**

When water and molecules in the air move slower, the weak attraction between them becomes greater and more air can dissolve in water.

When water that has air dissolved in it is warmed, the water and molecules in the air move faster. When water and molecules in the air move faster, the weak attraction between them is overcome. Then, molecules in the air start to collect together. A tiny air bubble forms when enough air molecules collect together. These tiny air bubbles that you should see are collections of air molecules that were dissolved in the water when the water was colder.

Sometimes water from lakes and rivers is used by industry for cooling purposes. When water is used to cool things, the water becomes warm. This warm water has less dissolved air in it. Sometimes the warm water is returned to the lake or river from where it came. If this warm water is returned directly to lakes and rivers, it can cause thermal pollution. Since there is less air in the warm water, there will be less air available for aquatic life in the rivers and lakes.

Other things to try

Repeat this experiment using warm water from a sink faucet. Do you see gas bubbles form in the water after several hours?

Fill a jar—with a tight fitting lid —half-full with cold water from your sink faucet. Add several ice cubes to the water. Attach the jar lid. Shake the water and ice cubes for one minute. Place the jar on the countertop or table. Let the jar sit for five minutes. Carefully pour the cold water into a tall clear glass. Place the glass in a warm spot where it will not be disturbed. Do you see gas bubbles clinging to the glass after several hours?

2 IS THERE GAS PRESSURE IN A CARBONATED DRINK?

Materials

A clear, carbonated drink in an unopened plastic bottle

Procedure

This experiment works best with a carbonated drink that is at room temperature. Remove the paper or plastic label around the plastic bottle to help you see the experiment better.

Gently squeeze the unopened bottle. Is the bottle firm? Observe the liquid in the unopened bottle. Do you see gas bubbles in the liquid? Now, open the bottle by unscrewing the cap until you hear a swishing sound coming from the bottle. Observe the liquid in the bottle. Gently squeeze the opened bottle. Screw the cap tightly back on the bottle. Observe the liquid in the bottle for thirty seconds. Gently squeeze the closed bottle after thirty seconds.

UNOPENED CARBONATED DRINK

OPENED CARBONATED DRINK

You may be able to repeat these steps several times with the same carbonated drink.

Observations

Is the plastic bottle containing the unopened carbonated drink firm when you squeeze it? Do you see many gas bubbles in the unopened drink?

Do you see gas bubbles form in the liquid when you open the drink? Do the gas bubbles move to the top of the bottle? Do some of the gas bubbles stick to the side of the bottle? Can you squeeze the sides of the opened bottle?

Do the gas bubbles stop forming in the liquid when you screw the cap tightly back on the bottle? Does the bottle become firm again after you secure the cap back on the bottle?

Discussion

Carbonated water is made by dissolving carbon dioxide molecules in water. When a drink containing carbonated water is bottled, additional carbon dioxide molecules are made to dissolve in the liquid. When the bottle is capped, some of the dissolved carbon dioxide molecules and some water molecules leave the liquid and become gases. These gases are trapped in the space above the liquid because the tightly secured bottle cap keeps the gas molecules from leaving the bottle. After the bottle has been capped for a few minutes and has reached an even temperature, the number of gaseous molecules in the space above the liquid remains the same and does not change.

The gas and liquid molecules in a carbonated drink are constantly moving. The moving gas molecules in the space above the liquid push on the sides of the drink bottle. The push due to the motion of molecules is called <u>pressure</u>. The more molecules there are in the gas space above the liquid, the greater the pressure of the gas. The gas pressure in a carbonated beverage is between thirty and forty-five pounds per square inch. This is greater than the pressure in the atmosphere, which is around fifteen pounds per square inch. The pressure in the carbonated drink is greater than the pressure of the atmosphere because of the additional carbon dioxide molecules which were added during the bottling of the drink. The unopened plastic bottle of carbonated drink should feel firm because of the increased gas pressure in the bottle.

In the unopened bottle of carbonated drink, some of the carbon dioxide molecules dissolved in the water and some of the water molecules move fast enough to leave the liquid and become a gas. These gaseous carbon dioxide molecules and water molecules move into the space above the liquid. When these molecules leave the liquid and become a gas, the same number of the slower moving gaseous carbon dioxide molecules and water molecules already in the space above the liquid move back into the liquid and become dissolved in the liquid. The number of molecules leaving the liquid and going into the gas space is balanced by the number of molecules in the gas space going back into the liquid. This balance of moving molecules is called <u>equilibrium</u>.

When the bottle cap is opened on the carbonated drink, the pressure in the bottle drops rapidly. The pressure drops because the gas molecules in the space above the liquid leave the bottle. When the pressure drops, the equilibrium between molecules leaving the liquid and the gas molecules redissolving in the liquid is changed. Now more carbon dioxide molecules leave the liquid and become a gas.

This is why you should see gas bubbles form and rise to the top of the bottle when you open the carbonated drink.

When you tightly reclose the cap on the carbonated drink, carbon dioxide molecules dissolved in the water will continue to leave the liquid and became a gas until the number of molecules leaving the liquid and going into the gas space is again balanced by the number of molecules in the gas space going back into the liquid. A new equilibrium is reached. This is why you should see carbon dioxide bubbles stop forming in the bottle soon after you tightly reclose the bottle.

Other things to try

Try the same experiment on other carbonated drinks in plastic bottles. Do you see similar results?

Try a cold carbonated drink. Do you see as many carbon dioxide bubbles when you first open the cold carbonated drink?

Try a carbonated drink in a glass bottle. You will not be able to squeeze the bottle. You should, however, be able to see gas bubbles form when you open it, and you should be able to see the gas bubbles stop forming when you secure the cap back on the bottle.

3 DOES A MIST FORM ABOVE THE LIQUID OF A CARBONATED DRINK WHEN IT IS OPENED?

Materials

A bottle opener

A cold, unopened carbonated drink in a clear glass bottle which has a crimped metal bottle cap

Procedure

You can use a cold, carbonated drink in a plastic bottle with a plastic screw cap. However, this experiment works best with a carbonated drink which is sealed with a crimped metal bottle cap.

Hold an unopened carbonated drink which is sealed with a crimped metal bottle cap firmly on a table. Look at the space above the liquid in the bottle. While you continue to look at the space above the liquid, use the bottle opener to quickly open the carbonated drink.

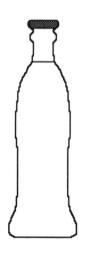

UNOPENED
CARBONATED
DRINK

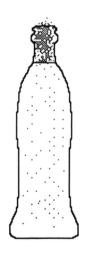

A CARBONATED
DRINK JUST
OPENED

Quickly make your observations because the mist may disappear rapidly.

Observations

Is the space above the liquid in the unopened drink bottle cloudy? Does the space above the liquid become cloudy or misty when you quickly open the drink bottle? How long does the mist last?

Discussion

Carbonated water is the major ingredient in all carbonated drinks. Carbonated water is made by dissolving carbon dioxide molecules in water. When a carbonated drink is bottled, additional carbon dioxide molecules are made to dissolve in the water. When the bottle is capped, some of the carbon dioxide molecules leave the liquid as a gas and collect in the space above the liquid. There are also some gaseous water molecules in the space above the liquid. The tightly-secured bottle cap keeps these gas molecules from leaving the bottle.

The gas molecules in the space above the liquid in an unopened carbonated drink are constantly moving. The moving gas molecules push on the sides of the drink bottle. The push due to the motion of molecules is called pressure. The gas pressure in a carbonated beverage is between thirty and forty-five pounds per square inch. This pressure is greater than the pressure in the atmosphere, which is around fifteen pounds per square inch. The pressure in the carbonated drink is greater than the pressure of the atmosphere because of the additional carbon dioxide molecules which were added during the bottling of the drink.

When the bottle cap is removed from the carbonated drink, the pressure in the bottle rapidly drops to the same pressure as the atmosphere. The pressure drops because the gas molecules in the space above the liquid leave the bottle. This loss of pressure causes the temperature in the space above the liquid to drop. The gaseous molecules in the space above the liquid become colder. The cold gaseous water molecules in the space above the liquid change from a gas into small droplets of liquid water and form a mist. A mist or cloud is formed from tiny drops of water that scatter light and appear white.

Other things to try

Try this experiment with other cold carbonated drinks in bottles with crimped metal bottle caps.

Repeat this experiment using a warm carbonated drink.

DOES MOVING AIR HAVE LESS PRESSURE THAN STILL AIR?

4

Materials

A hair dryer   A balloon

Procedure

HAVE AN ADULT HELP YOU WITH THIS EXPERIMENT. A HAIR DRYER SHOULD NEVER BE USED NEAR WATER OR PLACED IN WATER.

Blow up and tie the balloon. Plug in the hair dryer. Turn on the dryer. If there is a high setting, turn the dryer on high. Hold the dryer so that it blows straight up. Be careful, the air from the dryer will get hot. Use the cool air setting if the dryer has one. Hot air is not necessary for this experiment. Hold the balloon over the dryer and try pulling the balloon toward one side. Now let the balloon go. Watch the balloon.

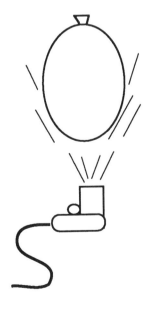

Observations

Does the balloon stay suspended in the moving air above the dryer? When you pull the balloon to the side, do you feel a pull against you? When you pull the balloon a little to the side and release the balloon, does the balloon move in the opposite direction? Does the balloon tend to stay in the middle of the air flow coming out of the dryer?

Discussion

Moving air has a lower pressure than stationary or still air. This observation is called the Bernoulli effect after the Swiss scientist Daniel Bernoulli who died in 1782. The Bernoulli effect explains why airplanes can fly.

Airplane wings are made into a shape called an air foil. Air that flows underneath an air foil wing goes slower than the air going above the wing. Air that goes above the wing goes farther and faster. Since faster moving air has less pressure than slower moving air, the pressure above the wing is less than below. This difference in pressure gives the plane an upward push. This upward push is called lift.

As a plane goes faster, the lift becomes greater. On takeoff a plane must go fast enough to cause a lift great enough to raise the plane off the ground.

Molecules in the air are moving in all directions. This random motion of air molecules is what creates air pressure. Molecules in air move hundreds of miles per hour in all directions. We are not aware of this motion because it is in all directions at once. We do feel the motion of air molecules from a hair dryer because all the molecules are moving in the same direction.

The balloon stays above the dryer because the molecules of air coming out of the dryer strike the bottom of the balloon and keep it from falling. When you pull on the balloon, there is a force that seems to tug the balloon back in the opposite direction. The pull is toward the side with the moving air that has a lower pressure.

Other things to try

Blow up a balloon. Tie a string on the balloon. Hold the balloon over the dryer. Let go of the balloon. Hold the string and pull the balloon to the side. Is the balloon pulled away so the string is stretched out straight?

Can you raise a balloon off the ground without touching it? Try blowing air across the top of the balloon. Does the balloon go up in the air?

5 CAN COOLING CAUSE A BALLOON TO GET SMALLER?

Materials

A large balloon	A pen
A refrigerator freezer	A ruler
A sink with a hot water faucet	A towel

Procedure

Blow up a balloon so it is about nine inches across. The balloon has to be able to fit into the freezer. Tie the balloon closed so no air leaks out.

Turn the hot water faucet on and hold the inflated balloon under the water for about three minutes. Be careful not to burn yourself with the hot water. Quickly dry one side of the balloon with the towel. Hold the ruler against the balloon. Make two marks on the balloon exactly two inches apart.

Now place the balloon in the refrigerator freezer. Wait about thirty minutes. Remove the balloon from the freezer. Hold the ruler against the balloon. Measure the exact distance between the two marks.

Observations

Are the two marks on the cold balloon still two inches apart? Did the two marks move closer together or farther apart? Do the marks move farther apart as the balloon warms?

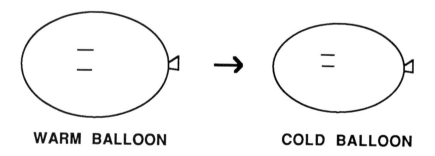

WARM BALLOON → COLD BALLOON

Discussion

Air is a gas and is made mostly of molecules of nitrogen and oxygen. Nitrogen and oxygen molecules are much too small to see. There are spaces between these molecules, and the molecules in air are always moving. In a balloon the molecules are constantly hitting each other and hitting the sides of the balloon.

When air becomes colder, air molecules move slower. When air becomes warmer, air molecules move faster. Faster moving gas molecules take up more room than slower moving gas molecules.

When you put the balloon under hot water, the air in the balloon expands. The air expands because the molecules are moving faster and take up more space. When you put the balloon in the freezer, the air gets cold. The balloon gets smaller because the air molecules move slower and take up less space. The two marks on the side of the balloon move closer together when the balloon gets smaller.

When you take the balloon out of the freezer, the cold air gets warmer and expands. As the balloon expands, the distance between the two marks on the balloon gets farther apart.

Other things to try

Try this experiment with two balloons of identical sizes. Put one balloon in the freezer and one under hot water. Wait about five minutes and then compare the sizes of the balloons. Hold the two balloons side by side. Can you see a change in the sizes of the balloons?

Repeat this experiment and measure the distance around the balloon with a string. How much does the distance around the balloon change when the balloon is warmed or cooled?

6 DOES SUGAR WATER EVAPORATE SLOWER THAN PURE WATER?

Materials

Three small plastic cups   A tablespoon
Sugar   Tape
Water   A felt pen

Procedure

It is best to do this experiment on a warm or hot sunny day.

Place a piece of tape on one of the plastic cups and use the felt pen to label the cup "water." Place a piece of tape on a second cup and label it "sugar water." Add one tablespoon of water to the cup labeled "water."

To make the sugar water, add one tablespoon of sugar and one tablespoon of water to the cup that is not labeled. Stir the sugar and water until all the sugar dissolves. Carefully measure one tablespoon of the sugar water and add it to the cup labeled "sugar water." You may rinse out the remaining sugar water in the cup that is not labeled.

Place the two labeled cups outside on a hot, sunny day where they will be in the sun for several hours and where they will not be disturbed. A window that gets plenty of sunshine may work also. Observe the liquid levels in the cups for several hours.

Observations

Does the water or sugar water start to disappear first? In which cup does all the water disappear first? Do you eventually see sugar crystals in the cup labeled "sugar water?" Does all the water finally disappear from the cup labeled "sugar water?"

WATER   SUGAR WATER

AFTER SEVERAL HOURS

Discussion

In this experiment water disappears from each cup by <u>evaporation</u>. Water changes from a liquid to a gas when it evaporates. Heat causes evaporation to occur faster. This is why you should do this experiment in a warm place.

In liquid water, individual water molecules are surrounded by other water molecules. The individual water molecules are attracted to each other. When water molecules are a gas, they are surrounded by empty space. There is very little attraction between gaseous water molecules.

When water evaporates, liquid water molecules must overcome the attractions of other water molecules around it. Liquid water molecules must move much faster than other molecules around them to break this attraction and evaporate. When molecules absorb heat they move faster.

In the cup labeled "sugar water," both water and table sugar molecules are present. The table sugar molecules slow the evaporation of water molecules from the cup. The sugar molecules do this by attracting some of the moving water molecules. These water molecules no longer have enough energy to overcome attractions of other water molecules. They no longer can change to a gas. This is why you should see the water in the cup labeled "water" evaporate faster than the water in the cup labeled "sugar water."

Table sugar molecules are too large to evaporate in this experiment. This is why you should see sugar crystals still remaining in the cup labeled "sugar water" when all the water has evaporated.

Other things to try

Repeat this experiment using different amounts of sugar. What do you observe?

DOES EVAPORATION OF MOLECULES CAUSE COOLING?

Materials

Two small clay flower pots	Ice
Two plastic plates	Water
Two small plastic bags	A bucket
Two small stones	

Procedure

You will need to do this experiment on a warm day. Fill the bucket with water. Place one of the clay pots in the bucket of water. Let the pot soak in the bucket of water overnight.

Fill each plastic bag with the same amount of ice. Close the plastic bags and seal with a metal twist or use Ziploc bags.

Place the plastic plates outside where the sun is shining. Put a bag of ice on each plate. Remove the clay pot from the bucket of water. Turn the clay pots upside down, and cover each bag of ice with a clay pot. One clay pot is dry and one is wet.

Pour a small layer of water on each plate. Cover the hole in the bottom of each pot with a small stone or rock. After about thirty minutes, raise each pot and compare the amount of ice left in each plastic bag.

After you have checked on the amount of ice under each pot, put the pots back over the bags of ice and continue the experiment. Every so often you can check on the bags to see how much ice has melted under each pot. How often you need to check on the ice will depend on how hot it is when you do this experiment.

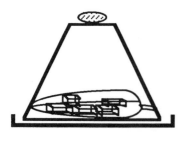 

DRY CLAY POT   **WET CLAY POT**

Observations

How much ice is left unmelted under the dry pot? How much ice is left unmelted under the wet pot? Touch each pot. Which one feels cooler? Under which pot does the ice last longer?

Discussion

Evaporation is the process by which a liquid changes to a gas. Since it takes energy to cause molecules to change from a liquid to a gas, evaporation results in cooling. The cooling is due to energy needed to separate the liquid molecules. The molecules with more energy leave the liquid, and the remaining molecules have less energy and are cooler on average.

Evaporation of water from the wet pot keeps it cooler than the dry pot. Since the wet pot is cooler, it takes longer for the ice to melt under the wet pot.

When the water in the wet clay pot evaporates, some water molecules gain enough energy to leave the pot and go into the air. The molecules are closer together as a liquid. The molecules are farther apart as a gas. When the water molecules become a gas they are spread throughout the air.

Other things to try

Compare how you feel on a day that is hot and humid with a day that is hot and dry. Generally we feel cooler when the weather is dry rather than humid. When the air is humid, there are a lot of water molecules in the air. On humid days, it is harder for the water on our skin to evaporate and make us cooler.

Compare how you feel on a day that is hot and breezy with a day that is hot with no breeze. Generally we feel cooler if the wind is blowing. As the wind blows across our skin, it helps water molecules evaporate. When we sweat, the moisture on our skin evaporates and helps keep us cool. Cats and dogs pant in hot weather and lose moisture from their tongues. This helps cats and dogs keep cool.

Does a wet or dry cloth feel cooler on a hot day? How can you find out?

8 DOES HEATING IN MICROWAVE OVENS REQUIRE WATER MOLECULES?

Materials

A microwave oven	Two metal spoons
A measuring cup	Two bowls
Sugar	Water

Procedure

ASK AN ADULT TO HELP YOU WITH THIS EXPERIMENT. NEVER PUT METAL INTO A MICROWAVE OVEN! NEVER HEAT A CLOSED CONTAINER IN A MICROWAVE OVEN. BE CAREFUL WHEN TOUCHING ANYTHING THAT HAS BEEN HEATED IN A MICROWAVE OVEN. IT MAY BE VERY HOT.

Make sure both bowls are clean and completely dry. Pour one-fourth cup of water into one bowl. Pour one-fourth cup of sugar into the second bowl. Place both bowls in a microwave oven. Close the microwave and heat on high for twenty seconds.

After twenty seconds of heating, turn off the microwave and then open the microwave. Remove both bowls from the microwave. Place a metal spoon in each bowl. Wait about twenty seconds and remove the spoons from the bowls. A spoon is used to make sure you do not get burned by touching something the microwave has made too hot. Carefully touch the part of the spoon that was in the sugar. Carefully touch the part of the spoon that was in the water.

Observations

Did the spoon in the water get hot? Did the spoon in the sugar get hot? Did the microwave oven heat the water? Did the microwave oven heat the sugar?

AFTER MICROWAVE HEATING

 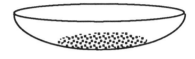

WATER HOT   **SUGAR NOT HOT**

Discussion

Microwave ovens generate <u>electromagnetic radiation</u>. Electromagnetic radiation is a form of energy. In a microwave oven, the energy of microwave radiation causes water molecules to rotate faster. The faster rotating molecules of water have more energy than slower rotating water molecules.

Food containing water cooks because the faster rotating water molecules cause other molecules to move more rapidly.

This energy of motion is called <u>heat</u>. The heat gradually spreads throughout the food. The food gets hot and cooks. Almost all food has water in it, and the rate of heating depends on the amount of water in the food.

In this experiment, the spoon in the water should become hot because the microwave energy heats the water in the bowl. The spoon in the sugar should not become hot because the sugar is dry.

Other things to try

Try adding water to the sugar and heating the water and sugar mixture for twenty seconds. Does the addition of the water cause microwave radiation to be absorbed? Does the sugar and water

33

mixture get hot? As you add more water to the originally dry sugar, is the mixture heated faster?

Pour a layer of water and a layer of cooking oil into a paper cup and place in the microwave oven. The oil layer will be on top. Place the cup in the microwave and heat for twenty seconds. Do not heat for more than twenty seconds. Remove the cup from the microwave and carefully touch the outside of the cup. Is the water layer hot? Is the oil layer hot? We expect that the layer of oil will not get as warm because it does not contain water. Of course, the heat will gradually spread throughout the cup over a period of time.

DOES WATER GO FROM A LIQUID TO A GAS WHEN POPCORN IS HEATED?

Materials

Popcorn (not microwave type)	A teaspoon
A stove	A bowl
A metal pan with lid	Water
Cooking oil	A paper towel

Procedure

Put two teaspoons of unpopped kernels of popcorn in a bowl. Fill the bowl with water until the popcorn is covered with water. Let the kernels of popcorn remain in the water overnight.

After soaking overnight, take the popcorn kernels from the bowl. Dry these popcorn kernels with a paper towel and set them aside.

GET AN ADULT TO HELP YOU WITH THIS PART OF THE EXPERIMENT. DO NOT USE THE STOVE BY YOURSELF. Turn a stove burner to high. Wait about five minutes until the burner becomes red hot. Be careful not to touch the hot part of the pan or stove.

Pour one teaspoon of oil into the pan. Add two teaspoons of regular, unsoaked popcorn kernels (kernels that have not soaked in water) to the pan. Cover the pan with a lid and place the pan on the stove. Leave pan lid slightly open to let steam escape. Wait several minutes and remove popcorn.

Pour one teaspoon of oil into the pan. Add two teaspoons of soaked popcorn kernels (dry kernels that have soaked in water overnight) to the pan. Cover the pan with a lid and place the pan on the stove. Leave pan lid slightly open to let steam escape. Wait several minutes and remove popcorn.

Observations

Do the regular kernels that have not been soaked in water change from small kernels into larger, fluffy white popcorn? Do the kernels that have been soaked in water change from small kernels into larger, fluffy white popcorn?

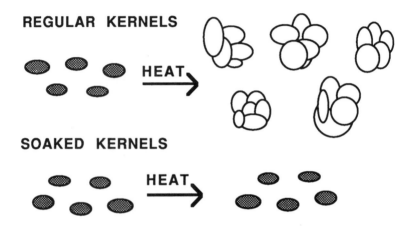

REGULAR KERNELS

HEAT →

SOAKED KERNELS

HEAT →

Discussion

Regular popcorn kernels are made of an inner layer of starch surrounded by a tough outer skin. Liquid water is trapped in the center of the kernel. When popcorn is heated, the water in the inner layer is changed to a gas (steam). As the gas expands and gas molecules push the starch apart, the softer starch material puffs up. As the kernel pops, the kernels swell apart, split, turn inside out, and break the outer seed coats.

Soaking kernels in water loosens the outer cover or skin of the popcorn kernel. When the kernel is heated, the water that is converted into steam is not trapped inside the kernel but can escape. Steam goes out into the air instead of causing the kernel to get bigger. Soaked kernels should not pop. Unsoaked kernels should pop.

Water boils at 100 degrees Celsius (212 degrees Fahrenheit). Water goes from a liquid to a gas on a hot stove. As molecules of water are heated, they change from a liquid to a gas. Liquid molecules are close together. Gas molecules are far apart.

Other things to try

Put two teaspoons of popcorn kernels in water and then take them out of water and dry them. Now try to pop these kernels. These kernels have been wet but did not soak in water. You should find that these kernels still pop normally because the outer layer has not been loosened.

You can repeat this experiment and try various soaking times to see how long the kernels must soak before they will no longer pop.

Heating must be rapid so water does not slowly escape from kernel. Try heating regular kernels of popcorn by slowly raising the temperature and see if the kernels pop.

Native Americans grew popcorn, and it is believed that popcorn was part of the first Thanksgiving feast. How do you think the Native Americans popped their popcorn?

10 CAN YOU FREEZE WATER WITH ICE?

Materials

A tall drinking glass

Ice

Table salt

Water

A measuring cup

A measuring spoon

A long spoon

A dish towel or paper towel

Procedure

Rinse the outside of a tall drinking glass with water. Do not dry the glass. You will freeze the water clinging to the outside of the glass in this experiment. Set the wet glass on a dish towel or paper towel. Add one-quarter cup of water to the glass. Use a measuring spoon to add three tablespoons of table salt to the glass. Stir the water and salt with a long spoon for fifteen seconds. Some of the salt will not dissolve.

Add five or six large ice cubes (seven or eight medium ice cubes) to the salt water. Stir the salt water and ice until the water on the outside of the glass freezes. You may have to stir several minutes for the water to freeze. If the ice cubes in the glass melt before the water on the outside of the glass freezes, add several more ice cubes.

**SALT ADDED TO
ICE WATER**

When you are done with the experiment, pour the salt water and ice down the drain of the sink. Rinse the sink with water.

Observations

How long does it take for the water clinging to the outside of the glass to freeze?

Discussion

A mixture of ice and pure water has a temperature of 0 degrees Celsius (32 degrees Fahrenheit). If the temperature is lowered below 0 degrees Celsius (32 degrees Fahrenheit), the liquid water changes to solid ice.

When table salt is added to ice water, the temperature of the salt water and ice mixture will drop below 0 degrees Celsius without the liquid salt water solution turning into solid ice. Salt lowers the freezing point of water below 0 degrees Celsius. If enough salt is added to ice water and the mixture is stirred, the temperature of the salt water and ice mixture can get as cold as -21 degrees Celsius (-6 degrees Fahrenheit).

In this experiment, the water clinging to the outside of your glass should freeze because the salt water and ice mixture inside the glass lowers the temperature of the outside of the glass below 0 degrees Celsius. The water on the outside of the glass changes to solid ice.

When only ice and water are in the glass, the temperature of the outside of the glass will not go below 0 degrees Celsius. The water on the outside of the glass will not freeze.

When a solid changes to a liquid, energy is absorbed, and this causes cooling. In a salt, ice, and water mixture this cooling occurs at a lower temperature. Salt lowers the temperature of the ice water mixture below 0 degrees Celsius by changing the melting process of ice. Salt changes the melting process of ice by making it more difficult for liquid water molecules to stick together and form ice. Because of this change, a mixture of salt, ice, and water stays as a liquid even below 0 degrees Celsius.

Other things to try

Repeat this experiment using no salt. Does the water clinging to the outside of the glass freeze? Repeat this experiment using one teaspoon of salt. Does the water clinging to the outside of the glass freeze?

DOES POPCORN DISSOLVE IN WATER? **11**

Materials

Popcorn	Water
Oil	Two bowls

Procedure

Use popcorn that has already been popped. Find two popped kernels of popcorn that are about the same size. Set one popped kernel on a plate. Put the second popped kernel in a bowl of water.

Observations

What happens to the popped kernel in the water? Wait several minutes and remove the popped kernel from the water. Compare this popped kernel to the one left on the plate. Which is smaller?

POPCORN KERNELS IN WATER

Discussion

The white, popped kernel of popcorn is made of two kinds of starch. Starch is made of large molecules that contain many sugar units connected together. The two kinds of starch in popcorn are amylose and amylopectin.

Amylose will dissolve in water. Amylopectin will not dissolve in water. The structure of these molecules are different. Amylose is made of long chains of 1,000 or more glucose sugar units. Amylopectin is made of highly branched molecules. Each molecule of amylopectin is made of several hundred short chains of twenty to twenty-five glucose units. The larger and more highly branched amylopectin will not break apart into the glucose sugar units from which it is made.

Expanding steam spreads out the starch in a popcorn kernel when popcorn is popped. Popped kernels are soft and fluffy. However, when popcorn is placed in water, it shrivels and gets smaller. Some of the popped kernel dissolves in water and some of it does not. The part of the popped kernel that dissolves is amylose. The part of the popped kernel that does not dissolve is amylopectin.

Other things to try

Repeat this experiment with two kernels of popcorn. Put one popped kernel in a bowl of cooking oil. Put the second popped kernel in a bowl of water. Does the popped kernel in the oil get smaller? Oil is nonpolar. Water is polar. Usually polar substances dissolve in polar liquids. Does this help explain the difference?

Repeat this experiment using a bowl of hot water and a bowl of cold water. Does the popped kernel dissolve more rapidly in the cold or hot water?

Place an unpopped kernel and a popped kernel in water. Does the unpopped kernel dissolve? Is the unpopped kernel covered with a protective coating that does not dissolve?

DOES SALT DISSOLVE MORE IN WATER OR IN RUBBING ALCOHOL? **12**

Materials

Two small jars   Water

Salt   Rubbing alcohol

Procedure

GET AN ADULT TO HELP YOU WITH THIS EXPERIMENT. CAUTION: DO NOT GET RUBBING ALCOHOL IN YOUR EYES OR MOUTH. RUBBING ALCOHOL IS NOT THE SAME TYPE OF ALCOHOL THAT IS FOUND IN ALCOHOLIC DRINKS. DO NOT DRINK IT. RUB-BING ALCOHOL IS POISON. KEEP AWAY FROM HEAT OR FLAMES.

Sprinkle a small amount of salt on the bottom of each jar. Pour enough water into one jar so that the bottom is covered in a layer about one-eighth inch deep (same height as two quarters stacked on top of each other). Pour enough rubbing alcohol into the second jar so that the bottom is covered in a layer about one-eighth inch deep. Cover this jar with a lid.

Swirl each jar. After you are finished with the experiment, pour the liquids down the drain and discard the jar that contained rubbing alcohol.

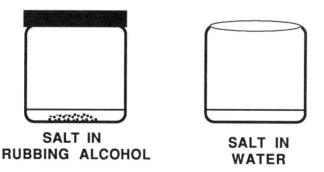

SALT IN RUBBING ALCOHOL   **SALT IN WATER**

Observations

Do you see small grains of salt in the bottom of each jar? As you swirl the jars, do the grains of salt disappear in the jar of water? Do grains of salt disappear in the covered jar of rubbing alcohol?

Discussion

Table salt is <u>sodium chloride</u>. Table salt is made of positive sodium ions and negative chlorine ions. When table salt is placed in water, it breaks apart into positive sodium ions and negative chlorine ions. The charged ions are surrounded by molecules of water. Water molecules have a positive and negative side and are said to be polar.

Rubbing alcohol is a molecule called <u>isopropyl alcohol</u>. Each isopropyl alcohol molecule contains a nonpolar part with three carbon atoms and seven hydrogen atoms, and a polar part with one hydrogen and one oxygen. The polar part is like water. Water contains two hydrogen atoms and one oxygen atom. The nonpolar part of isopropyl alcohol is more like oil. Oil is nonpolar.

Because isopropyl alcohol is not as polar as water, table salt does not dissolve as readily in rubbing alcohol as in water. Rubbing alcohol is often sold as a mixture of 70 percent isopropyl alcohol and 30 percent water.

Other things to try

Try adding table salt to oil. Does the salt dissolve in oil? Can you explain your observations?

Try adding food coloring to water and food coloring to isopropyl alcohol. Food coloring molecules have a polar and a nonpolar part so we might expect them to dissolve in both types of liquids. Does the food coloring dissolve in both liquids and color both liquids? CAUTION: DO NOT GET RUBBING ALCOHOL IN EYES OR IN MOUTH.

Try adding salt to liquid detergent. Does salt dissolve? Liquid detergent contains water and soap molecules. Soap molecules have a polar and a nonpolar end. The presence of soap may make the salt dissolve more slowly.

Compare the time it takes salt to dissolve in water with mixtures of various amounts of liquid detergent added.

13 CAN MOLECULES OF WATER HOLD GRAINS OF SAND TOGETHER?

Materials

Dry sand (the white sand used in sandboxes works well)

A teaspoon   A paper cup   Water

Procedure

Fill a small paper cup about one-half full with dry sand. Try pushing one finger straight down in the sand.

Gently pour five teaspoons of water on the top of the sand. The top of the sand will now be slightly wet. Try pushing one finger straight down into the sand.

Observations

How far can you push your finger into the dry sand? How far can you push your finger into the wet sand? Does the dry or wet sand feel firmer? Is it harder to push your finger into dry or wet sand?

Discussion

You should find that you can push your finger deeper into dry sand than the slightly wet sand. You should find it much harder to push your finger down into wet sand. The wet sand feels firmer.

Sand is made of tiny grains. The grains of sand are made of silicon dioxide. Silicon dioxide is made of silicon and oxygen atoms. Each grain of sand consists of billions and billions of silicon and oxygen atoms.

Water is made of individual molecules. Each water molecule is made of one oxygen atom and two hydrogen atoms. Molecules of water are attracted to the surface of grains of sand. The water molecules get between grains of sand and help hold them together.

Grains of sand are pulled together by water. The water molecules are attracted to each other and to the sand. The water molecules try

DRY SAND - SOFT   WET SAND - FIRM

to pull together. Water molecules also pull the grains of sand together. This tendency of water molecules to pull together is called <u>surface tension</u>.

Surface tension causes water to form beads on a waxed car. Water molecules on the surface of the drop are pulled back toward the middle of the drop. Drops of water do not spread out on a surface like a waxed car.

Dry sand falls apart. Sand put under water falls apart. However, sand that is slightly wet stays together. Grains of sand are wet from the water. To make clumps of sand stay together, you need sand that is neither too wet nor too dry.

Other things to try

Lift up a clump of sand from your cup. Does it stick together? Try doing the same with dry sand. Will it stick together? Put the clump of wet sand into a bucket filled with water. Does it stay together or fall apart?

Add more water to your cup of sand and keep trying to push your finger down into the sand. As water begins to stand on top of the sand, is easier to push your finger down into the sand?

Have you ever walked along a sandy beach at the ocean? Did you notice that it is much harder to walk in the dry sand than wet sand? In dry sand your feet sink down, but on wet sand, near the edge of the water, you can walk and your feet don't sink down into the sand. Can you explain why?

14 CAN OIL HELP YOU SEE THROUGH PAPER?

Materials

A sheet of newspaper with printing

A piece of notebook paper   Cooking oil

Procedure

Place a piece of newspaper on a table. Next place a piece of notebook paper flat on the newspaper. Try to read the newspaper that is directly under the notebook paper.

Put one or two drops of cooking oil in the center of the notebook paper. Spread the oil out in a circle about the size of your fist using your fingers. Now try to read the newspaper that is directly under the oil spot on the notebook paper.

Observations

Can you read the newspaper that is directly under the notebook paper when no oil is on the paper? Is it easier to read the newspaper that is directly under the oil spot on the notebook paper?

**PAPER WITH
OIL ON IT**

**PAPER WITH
NO OIL ON IT**

48

Discussion

Notebook paper is made of many layers of tiny fibers. Tear a piece of paper and look at the tear. You should be able to see the many individual fibers in the layers that make up the paper. The spaces between the fibers contain air.

When light passes through substances, it can be changed. The light's speed can change and light can go in many different directions. Light is said to be <u>scattered</u> when it is made to go in many different directions.

As light passes through paper its speed is constantly changing as it moves through the layers of fiber and air in the paper. Because the light is scattered as it passes through the notebook paper, it is difficult to read the newspaper that is underneath.

When oil is added to the paper, oil molecules move into the spaces between the fibers and force the air molecules out. Light passes through oil and paper fibers at about the same speed. There is little scattering of the light when it passes through the oil and paper fiber layers. Because the light does not scatter, it is easier to read the newspaper directly under the oil spot on the notebook paper.

Other things to try

Repeat this experiment using a piece of paper cut from a brown grocery bag. Do you get similar results? Try other types of paper and other types of oils.

Look at a newspaper through a piece of wax paper. Can you see through the wax paper? Wax paper is made by squeezing wax molecules into the spaces between the paper fibers. Light passes through layers of wax and paper fibers at about the same speed.

15 DOES A LIQUID DETERGENT TURN CLOUDY WHEN IT BECOMES COLD?

Materials

Two clear plastic cups   A refrigerator freezer

A measuring cup   Corn syrup

Tape   A felt pen

A clear, liquid dishwashing detergent such as Ajax or Dawn

Procedure

Put a piece of tape on each cup. Use the pen to label one cup "detergent" and the other cup "corn syrup." Make sure to write on the tape.

Pour one-quarter cup of clear, liquid, dishwashing detergent into the cup labeled "detergent." Pour one-quarter cup of corn syrup in the cup labeled "corn syrup." Place the two cups in a refrigerator freezer. Leave them in the freezer overnight. The next day remove the cups from the freezer and make your observations.

Observations

Are the liquid detergent and the corn syrup clear before you put them in the freezer? Does the liquid detergent become cloudy in the freezer? Does the corn syrup become cloudy in the freezer? Does the cold detergent still pour? Does the cold corn syrup still pour?

Discussion

Liquid dishwashing detergent contains detergent molecules dissolved in water. Detergent molecules are large molecules made of many carbon and hydrogen atoms. Detergent molecules also contain oxygen and sulfur atoms.

When detergent molecules dissolve in water, the detergent molecules become surrounded by many water molecules. As liquid

**WARM LIQUID
DETERGENT**

**COLD LIQUID
DETERGENT**

dishwashing detergent becomes cold, the individual detergent molecules start sticking to each other and clumping together.

The clumps of detergent molecules cause light to be deflected and scattered as the light passes through the cold liquid dishwashing detergent. This deflection of light by the clumps of detergent molecules causes the liquid dishwashing detergent to look cloudy. Liquid dishwashing detergent at room temperature is clear because the detergent molecules are surrounded by water molecules and do not clump together. The individual detergent molecules and water molecules are too small to deflect light very much.

Corn syrup contains corn sugar molecules dissolved in water. Corn syrup should not become cloudy when cooled in a freezer. The corn sugar molecules do not clump together. The corn sugar molecules remain surrounded by water molecules even when cold.

Other things to try

Set the cup of cold liquid detergent in a warm place like a window that gets plenty of sunshine. Does the cloudy liquid detergent become clear when it warms up?

Repeat this experiment with other clear liquid detergents to see if they become cloudy when they are made cold.

16 DOES LIGHT CHANGE WHEN IT PASSES THROUGH SUBSTANCES?

Materials

A bright flashlight   A two-cup measuring cup

Lowfat (2%) milk   A one-quarter cup measuring cup

A tall clear glass   A measuring spoon

Procedure

Fill a two-cup measuring cup with water. Add one-half teaspoon of lowfat (2%) milk to the two cups of water. Stir the milk and water with the measuring spoon. Observe the color of the milky solution.

Add one-quarter cup of the milky water to a tall clear glass. Take the flashlight and the glass of milky water into a dark room. Turn on the flashlight and shine the light through the bottom of the glass. You may need to put the flashlight against the glass. Look through the side of the glass. Observe the color of the light. Look through the top of the glass down at the flashlight. Observe the color of the light.

Add another one-quarter cup of the milky water to the glass. Again observe the color of the light from the flashlight from the side and above the glass. Continue adding one-quarter cup of the milky water and observing the color of the light until the glass is nearly full.

Observations

Is the milk and water solution clear or cloudy? Does the milk and water solution have a slight bluish color? Is the light beam slightly bluish in color when you observe the light beam from the side of the glass? Is the flashlight light bulb slightly red-orange in color when you look through at it from the top of the glass of the milky water? Does the flashlight light bulb become more red in color each time you add another one-quarter cup of the milky water to the glass?

MILK AND WATER

FLASHLIGHT

Discussion

Light from an <u>incandescent</u> light bulb contains all the colors of the rainbow. These colors are violet, indigo, blue, green, yellow, orange, and red. Light that contains all these colors is called <u>white light</u>.

Light is scattered when it passes through a substance. Light is scattered by particles. The particles can be atoms, molecules, or groups of atoms and molecules. When light is scattered, it goes in many different directions. Some colors of white light can be scattered more than others.

When white light from a flashlight is passed through milky water, the light is scattered by groups of large fat and protein molecules in the milk. The blue light is scattered more than the other colors. This is why milky water looks slightly bluish when you view the glass from the side. Red light is scattered the least of all the colors in white light by the groups of fat and protein molecules in milk. This is why the flashlight light bulb should appear reddish when you look at it directly through the milky water. As more milky water is added to the glass, the light is scattered by more fat and protein molecules, and the light bulb should appear more red.

This experiment can explain why the sky is blue and sunsets can be red. When light from the sun passes through the earth's atmosphere, air molecules, water molecules, and dust particles in the atmosphere cause the blue light of the sun to be scattered. When the blue light is scattered, it moves in all directions. This is why a clear sky appears bright and blue during the day. If none of the sun's light were scattered, then the sky would appear black. This is why objects in photos made in outer space appear to be on a black background.

At sunset the sun and the surrounding sky appear red because we are viewing the sun more directly. This means we are viewing more of a direct beam of light from the sun. Since the blue light of the sun is scattered by the atmosphere and little reaches our eyes, the sun's light appears reddish.

Other things to try

In a dark room, shine the light from a flashlight through several pieces of white notebook paper or typing paper. Does the light coming through the paper appear red? Does the light coming through the paper become redder if you shine the light through several more sheets of paper?

CAN WATER SEPARATE LIGHT INTO DIFFERENT COLORS?

17

Materials

A garden water hose

An adjustable nozzle for the hose

Procedure

This experiment must be done outside when the sun is shining. ASK AN ADULT TO HELP YOU WITH THIS EXPERIMENT. Make sure to turn off the water to the garden hose when you are finished with the experiment.

Turn the water on to a garden hose that has an adjustable nozzle attached to it. Stand with your back facing the sun. Open the nozzle to the water hose just until you get a fine mist. Spray the mist in front of yourself. If you do not see a rainbow in the spray, move the spray of fine mist up and down in front of yourself.

While spraying water from the nozzle and while holding the nozzle in front of you, rotate your body until you are facing the sun. Do you still see a rainbow?

RAINBOW IN WATER SPRAY

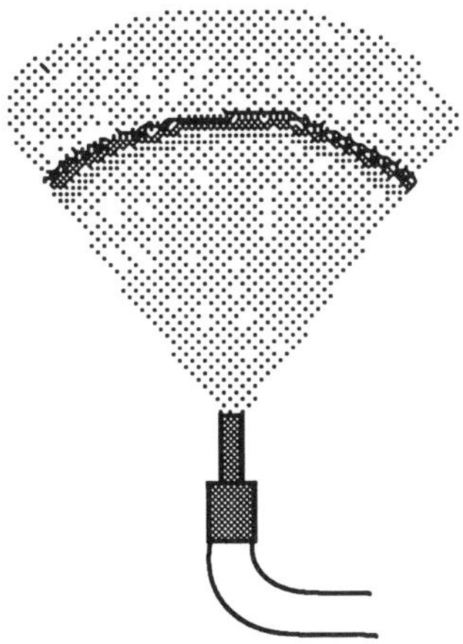

Observations

What colors do you see in the rainbow? Do you see a rainbow in the water spray when the sun is behind you? Do you see a rainbow in the water spray when you are facing the sun?

Discussion

Sunlight appears white, but it is actually made of the colors violet, indigo, blue, green, yellow, orange, and red. Light that contains all these colors is called white light.

Sunlight, or white light, can be separated into different colors. One way to do this is by passing the light through a prism. A prism is a geometrical shape usually made of glass. When white light passes through a prism, the different colors of light pass through the prism at different speeds. This causes the different colors to become separated. The separation of white light into different colors is called dispersion.

The collection of water molecules in raindrops can act like tiny prisms. When sunlight passes through raindrops, the white light is separated into different colors because the different colors of light pass through the collection of water molecules at different speeds. In addition, some of the separated light is reflected back and passes through the front of the raindrops. This is why we see a rainbow when the sun is behind us.

Other things to try

Adjust the nozzle until the water spray is made of large drops of water. Do you still see a rainbow when your back is facing the sun?

Hold the spray of water at different angles from the sun. What angle makes the brightest and best rainbow?

CAN YOU SEE SEPARATE COLORS WHEN YOU LOOK AT A MERCURY STREETLIGHT WITH A COMPACT DISC? **18**

Materials

A music compact disc (CD)   An incandescent lamp
Mercury streetlight

Procedure

ASK AN ADULT TO HELP YOU WITH THIS EXPERIMENT. DO NOT STAND IN THE STREET WHILE MAKING YOUR OBSERVATIONS.

Most streetlights use either mercury or sodium vapor lamps as their light source. Streetlights that are yellow-orange in color are probably sodium vapor lamps. Streetlights that are bluish white in color are probably mercury lamps. For the main part of this experiment you will want to use a mercury streetlight.

Remove the CD from its case. Notice that there is printing on one side of the CD. Place the CD back in the case so that the side with the printing is face down in the holder. The side with no printing should be facing up. This will help you make your observations.

It is best to do this experiment when it is dark. Go into a room that has an incandescent light. A table lamp or an overhead light should work. Turn the light on and stand facing the light. Stay as far away from the light as you can. Hold the back of the case with the CD flat on your stomach. Slowly tilt the bottom of the case up (the end of the case below your hands will move up) until you see a reflected image of the light in the CD. You should view the light with the CD along the imaginary line from the light to your body. Closing one eye may help you make observations. Continue to slowly tilt the bottom of the case up. You should see continuous colors as in a rainbow.

Go outside when it is dark and find a lit streetlight that does not have many other lights around it. Stand approximately twenty to sixty yards away from the streetlight. While facing the streetlight, tilt the CD case up and down as you did before and make your observations.

Observations

Do you see continuous colors of light when you look at an incandescent light with a CD? Do you see continuous or separate colors of light when you look at a mercury streetlight with a CD?

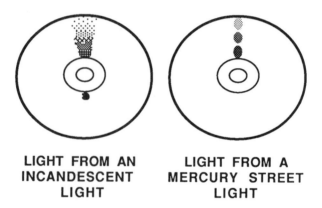

| LIGHT FROM AN INCANDESCENT LIGHT | LIGHT FROM A MERCURY STREET LIGHT |

Discussion

Light from the sun and <u>incandescent</u> light bulbs is called white light because it appears white to our eyes. <u>White light</u> from the sun and incandescent light bulbs is actually a mixture of many different colors of light. These colors are the colors of the rainbow. They are violet, indigo, blue, green, yellow, orange, and red. When you view a rainbow you are seeing the white light of the sun being separated into these individual colors by raindrops in the air. The raindrops act like tiny prisms. A prism is a geometrical shape usually made of glass that can separate white light into a number of different colors. Light separated into different colors is called a <u>spectrum</u>.

A <u>grating</u> can also separate white light into a number of different colors of light. A grating consists of very narrow, closely spaced lines that are parallel to each other. There can be thousands of these narrow lines in an inch in some gratings. When light is separated into a number of different colors by a grating process it is called <u>diffraction</u>.

A CD can be used as a grating. The grating pattern in a CD results from microscopic pits on the CD that appear as lines. These microscopic pits contain the music and information for the CD player. Remarkably, a human hair can cover sixty of the narrow lines of the microscopic pits on a CD.

When you look at an incandescent light with a CD, you should see the light separated into the colors of the rainbow. You should also not see any dark regions between the colors. This is called a continuous spectrum.

When you look at a mercury streetlight with a CD, you should see only regions of yellow, green, indigo, and violet. A faint region of orange-red may also be seen on the CD. You should also be able to see dark regions between the colors. You should also observe that the blue region is no longer present. The mercury streetlight appears bluish-white because the individual colors in the mercury streetlight mix together to give a bluish-white color.

The individual colors in the mercury streetlight are caused by changes in electrons in mercury atoms. Electrons are negatively charged particles that spin around the nucleus of an atom. When electrons absorb energy, they change to a higher energy level. When electrons release energy, they change back to a lower energy level.

The individual colors of light from the mercury streetlight are caused by electrons in the mercury atoms of the streetlight changing back to a lower energy level.

Other things to try

Repeat this experiment by looking at a sodium vapor streetlight. Streetlights that are yellow-orange in color are probably sodium vapor lamps. You will probably see all the colors of the rainbow, but you should notice the yellow colors of light are more bright and intense.

CAN LIGHT BE MADE WHEN TAPE IS PULLED?

19

Materials

A roll of electrical tape or duct tape

Procedure

This experiment works best when the humidity is low and the air is dry. Usually the best time to do this experiment is in the winter when it is cold and the humidity is low.

Unroll about an inch of the tape from the roll. Go into a dark room with the roll of tape. Make sure the room is totally dark. Wait at least one minute to allow your eyes to adjust to the darkness. While looking very closely at the underside of the tape where it sticks to the roll, pull the tape quickly to unroll several inches of tape. You must look carefully at the tape to see the light. If you do not see any light, the air may be too humid.

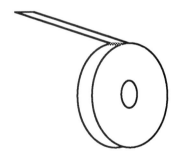

ROLL OF TAPE

Observations

Do you see a line of light where the tape separates from the roll when you pull the tape quickly? What color is the light? How long does the light last?

Discussion

Light is a form of energy. Some other forms of energy include heat, electrical energy, sound, chemical energy, and mechanical energy. Energy can be changed from one form to another form. For example, electrical energy (electricity) is converted into light and heat energy in a light bulb. Chemical energy in wood is converted into heat and light energy when wood burns.

In this experiment mechanical energy is converted into light energy. When you pull (mechanical energy) on the tape, the sticky adhesive on the underside of the tape separates from the backside of the tape under it. Molecules in the air near the sticky adhesive obtain extra energy when the adhesive separates from the backside of the tape under it. Molecules that contain extra energy are called excited molecules. The excited molecules in air quickly give off their extra energy as light. When the molecules in air give off their extra energy as light, they are no longer excited.

Other things to try

Repeat this experiment with other types of tape. Do you see similar results?

Can you explain how electrical energy in lightning causes light to be given off by molecules in air?

CAN A BALLOON CAUSE A FLUORESCENT BULB TO GIVE OFF LIGHT?

20

Materials

A balloon

A fluorescent light bulb

A dark room

Procedure

HAVE AN ADULT HELP YOU WITH THIS EXPERIMENT. HAVE AN ADULT HOLD THE FLUORESCENT BULB. BE CAREFUL NOT TO DROP OR BREAK THE BULB. NEVER USE HOUSE CURRENT (electricity from wall outlet) FOR THIS EXPERIMENT.

This experiment works best in the winter when the air is dry.

Blow up a balloon and tie it closed. Rub the balloon in your hair or on a sweater for about thirty seconds.

Turn off the lights so you are in a room that is completely dark. Now move the balloon until it touches the middle of the fluorescent bulb. Make your observations.

Observations

What do you see as the balloon touches the fluorescent bulb? Does the fluorescent bulb give off light?

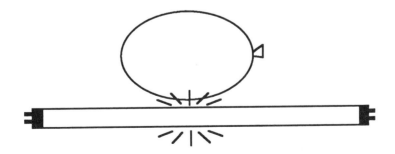

Discussion

Atoms are made of a positive nucleus surrounded by negative electrons. The electrons move around the nucleus and are located in a certain space around the nucleus we call an orbital.

When you rub a balloon on a sweater or in your hair, some electrons from the sweater move onto the balloon. The extra electrons on the balloon are called static electricity. When the balloon gets close to the bulb, some of the extra electrons flow from the balloon into the bulb.

In the normal operations of a fluorescent bulb, electrons flow through a wire at the end of the tube. Extra electrons are given off by this wire. These electrons hit mercury atoms in the gas in the tube. When the electrons hit the mercury atoms, they give off ultraviolet light. The ultraviolet light hits a special fluorescent coating on the inside of the tube. It is this fluorescent coating that gives off the white light that we see.

The electrons in the atoms of the fluorescent coating go to a higher energy orbital when struck by ultraviolet light. As the electrons go back to a lower energy orbital, they give off visible or white light.

In incandescent lights, a tungsten wire is heated to over 2,000 degrees Celsius from a flow of electrons through the wire. The heat energy causes light to be given off.

In incandescent bulbs much of the electrical energy is converted to heat rather than light. Fluorescent bulbs do not get as hot as incandescent bulbs. Fluorescent bulbs are more efficient at converting energy to light.

Other things to try

Try using a comb to generate light. Rapidly comb your hair for about fifteen seconds, then touch the comb to the fluorescent tube. Is light given off?

Try just holding a charged balloon near the tube and moving the balloon rapidly up and down. Does the tube light up?

IS CHEWING GUM LESS FLEXIBLE WHEN COLD?

21

Materials

Two sticks of gum   A refrigerator freezer

Procedure

Remove each stick of gum from its wrapper. Place one stick of gum in the freezer section of the refrigerator. Leave the other stick of gum out in the room. Wait twenty minutes.

Hold the warmer stick of gum by each end. Slowly move your hands together so that you bend this piece of chewing gum. Hold the colder stick of gum by each end. Slowly move your hands together so that you bend this piece of chewing gum.

Observations

Does the warmer stick of gum stay in one piece or break in two pieces? Does the colder stick of gum stay in one piece or break in two pieces? Is the colder or warmer gum able to bend more without breaking? Which stick of gum is more flexible?

COLD GUM

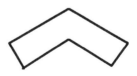

WARM GUM

Discussion

Chicle is a natural gum base made from boiling the milky juice of the Sapodilla tree which grows in Mexico and Central America.

General Santa Anna, who defeated the defenders of the Alamo in 1836, took chicle to a New York chemist named Thomas Adams in 1860. Adams boiled chicle and discovered it made a good substance to chew. Adams began to manufacture and sell chewing gum in the United States.

Chewing gum is made of sugar, gum base, softeners, flavors, and colors. Today most gum base for chewing is made artificially rather than from plants. In sugar-free gum, artificial sweeteners replace sugar. Softeners help the gum retain water when you chew it so the gum will not be too hard. Gum base is made of polymer molecules.

Polymer molecules are made of thousands of smaller molecules. The smaller molecules are connected together to make long polymer molecules.

Some polymers are rigid and stiff, like a plastic bottle. Other polymers are flexible and can be stretched like a rubber band.

Long chains of polymer molecules in chewing gum can bend without breaking if they are not too cold. When the molecules in the gum base in chewing gum become cold enough, the collection of molecules change from being flexible to being stiff and rigid. When the gum is warm, the molecules are free to move past each other. When the gum is cold enough, the molecules are not free to move past each other. The gum becomes brittle.

Warm chewing gum is flexible and will not break when bent. Cold chewing gum is not flexible and will break when bent. Chewing gum from a freezer snaps when you try to bend it.

Other things to try

Allow a piece of gum that has been in the freezer to warm back up to the temperature of the room. Is this piece of gum any different than one that has never been in the freezer? Will both pieces bend rather than break? Try freezing and warming different pieces of gum and testing their flexibility.

Repeat this experiment with different brands of chewing gum. Is there any difference in flexibility between gum that contains sugar and gum that is sugar free? Does the flexibility only depend on the polymer molecules in gum base? Does the presence of sugar make any difference in whether the gum bends or breaks?

Put a piece of gum in the refrigerator but not in the freezer and let it get cold. Now try bending this piece of gum. Is it cold enough to snap in two pieces or does it need to be colder?

22 IS CHEWING GUM LESS STICKY WHEN COLD?

Materials

Two sticks of gum   A bowl
A refrigerator freezer   A plate
Water

Procedure

Remove each stick of gum from its wrapper. Put both sticks of gum in a bowl of water, and let each soak for several minutes. After each piece of gum is wet, roll each piece into a ball. Squeeze the gum with your fingers until each piece of gum feels like moist, chewed gum.

Place one wet ball of gum in the freezer section of the refrigerator. Set the other ball of wet gum on a plate in the room. Wait about ten minutes.

Remove the gum from the freezer. Place the cold ball of gum between the thumb and finger of your left hand. Place the warm ball of gum between the thumb and finger of your right hand. Squeeze each piece of gum and then pull your thumb and finger apart.

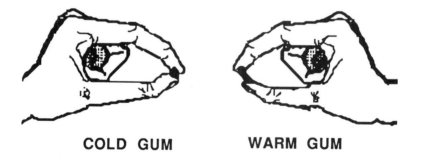

COLD GUM   WARM GUM

Next try to put each piece of gum on a plate and turn the plate upside down.

Observations

Is the warmer piece of gum sticky? Is the colder piece of gum sticky? Which piece feels more sticky? Do both pieces of gum stick to the plate?

Discussion

Two things, like your finger and thumb, can be stuck together by something that acts like an <u>adhesive</u>. For an adhesive substance to stick on a surface, the adhesive must wet the surface. Wetting the surface means that the substance completely covers the surface. The surface may be rough and uneven.

Long chains of polymer molecules in chewing gum can bend without breaking if they are not too cold. When the molecules in the gum base in chewing gum become cold, the molecules change from being flexible to being stiff and rigid.

Forces between the atoms on the surface and the atoms and molecules in the gum hold the gum on the surface of an object like your finger. When the gum is frozen, the water molecules in the gum are not free to flow. Also the large molecules in the gum are locked into position and are not able to be flexible and move. Since the frozen gum cannot wet the surface, cold gum is not as sticky as warm gum.

Other things to try

Put a piece of wet gum in the refrigerator but not in the freezer. Put another piece of wet gum in the freezer. Wait ten minutes while both pieces get cold. Which piece of gum is stickier?

A dry piece of gum will not stick on a surface. The gum must be wet for the gum to stick to something. Can you do an experiment to show that gum must be wet to be sticky?

Try wetting a piece of gum in cooking oil instead of water. Does this piece of gum get sticky or is water needed?

Put a wet ball of gum on a plate and heat the plate in a microwave oven for about ten to fifteen seconds. GET AN ADULT TO HELP YOU WITH THIS EXPERIMENT. NEVER PUT METAL IN A MICROWAVE OVEN! BE CAREFUL NOT TO TOUCH THE GUM; IT MAY GET VERY HOT! Remove the plate from the microwave and push a spoon against the gum and then pull on the spoon. Is this hot piece of gum very sticky? Does the gum stretch if you continue to pull on the spoon?

CAN THE SURFACE OF EGG YOLKS TURN GREEN DURING COOKING?

Materials

Two eggs

A small saucepan

Water

A watch or cooking timer

A bowl

A spoon

A stove

A knife

Procedure

ASK AN ADULT TO HELP YOU WITH THIS EXPERIMENT. DO NOT USE THE STOVE BY YOURSELF.

Place two eggs in a small saucepan. Cover the eggs with cold water from a sink faucet. Using high heat, heat the saucepan on a stove until the water starts to boil. Reduce the heat to low and continue cooking the eggs for twelve minutes.

After twelve minutes of cooking, remove one of the eggs with a spoon and put it in a bowl. Cover this egg with cold water from a sink faucet. Continue cooking the remaining egg in the saucepan for an additional fifteen minutes. Remove the second egg from the saucepan using a spoon and place this egg on the table to cool. Allow this egg to cool for thirty minutes.

Remove the shell from the egg that was cooked for twelve minutes and cooled in the cold water. Carefully cut the egg in half with a knife and then remove each half of the egg yolk. Observe the color of the outside of the yolk halves.

Remove the shell from the other egg and cut the egg in half with the knife. Remove each half of the egg yolk and observe the color of the outside of the yolk halves.

EGG YOLKS FROM HARD BOILED EGGS

**COOKED
12 MINUTES**

**COOKED
27 MINUTES**

Observations

Are the egg yolks of both eggs firm when you remove them from the egg whites? What color are the surfaces of the egg yolks? Is the surface of the egg yolk from the egg that was cooked longer greener in color than the egg that was cooked only twelve minutes? Is the green color just on the surface of the yolk or is the green color also inside the egg yolk?

Discussion

Chicken eggs contain a yellow egg yolk surrounded by the egg white. The egg yolk is a complex mixture of water, fats, and protein. The yolk also contains the minerals iron, calcium, and sodium.

The egg white is mostly water with some protein molecules dissolved in the water. <u>Protein</u> are large molecules important to living things. Protein molecules are made from smaller molecules called <u>amino acids</u>. Amino acids are linked together in long chains to make protein molecules.

The egg white cooks first when an egg is cooked in its shell. When the egg white cooks, the protein molecules in the egg white start to stick to each other. The egg white protein molecules continue to stick together until the egg white becomes semisolid. The protein molecules in the egg yolk stick together also to form a semisolid as the yolk cooks.

Some of the amino acids that are linked together in egg white proteins contain sulfur atoms. In the cooking process some of the sulfur atoms in the protein are changed into a new chemical substance called hydrogen sulfide. Hydrogen sulfide is a gas.

Some of the hydrogen sulfide gas that forms moves toward the center of the egg. When the hydrogen sulfide comes into contact with the egg yolk, the hydrogen sulfide combines with iron atoms on the surface of the egg yolk to make a new chemical substance called iron sulfide. Iron sulfide is a dark color and gives egg yolks a green color when the eggs have been cooked a long time.

In this experiment, the egg that was cooked for only twelve minutes should have very little green color on its yolk. The hydrogen sulfide generated in the cooking of this egg should not have had enough time to move to the center of the egg.

The egg that was cooked for a total time of twenty-seven minutes should have a green color on its egg yolk since more time was allowed for the hydrogen sulfide to move to the egg yolk.

Other things to try

Will egg yolks become greener in color the longer you cook the eggs? How can you find out?

24 CAN A FOAM BE MADE FROM EGG WHITE?

Materials

An egg

A small bowl

A hand beater or electric beater

Procedure

ASK AN ADULT TO HELP YOU WITH THIS EXPERIMENT. DO NOT USE AN ELECTRIC BEATER BY YOURSELF.

Remove an egg from the refrigerator. Allow it to warm to room temperature. This may take several hours. This experiment works best with an egg at room temperature.

You must separate the egg white from the yolk of the egg. To do this hold the egg in one hand and strike the middle of the egg on the edge of the bowl sharply enough to crack the egg. Grasp the cracked egg with both hands. Hold the cracked side of the egg up. Carefully open the egg shell with your hands. You may want to use your thumbs to help you pry the cracked egg shell apart. Continue to open the eggshell until the egg shell is broken in half.

Some of the egg white will flow from the open egg, so make sure to open the egg over the bowl. Also, make sure the egg yolk stays in one of the half egg shells. You must not get any egg yolk in the bowl with your egg white. Now carefully pour the egg yolk back and forth from one half egg shell to the other about three times. Some of the remaining egg white will flow into the bowl each time your pour the egg yolk back and forth. Place the egg yolk in a separate container. Ask an adult if he or she would like to use the separated egg yolk in cooking.

Start to beat the egg white with a hand beater or an electric beater. Observe the size of the air bubbles in the egg white as you beat them. Continue beating the egg whites until you form a firm, white foam. This may take a couple of minutes.

A FOAM MADE WITH EGG WHITES

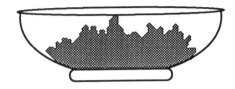

Observations

Is the egg white clear or cloudy before you start to beat it? Do air bubbles form in the egg white as you beat it? Do the air bubbles start out large and then become smaller as you continue to beat the egg white? When the egg white becomes a firm, white foam, is it clear or cloudy? How long does the foam last?

Discussion

Egg white is a mixture of mostly water and protein. For every eighty-eight water molecules in an egg white (88 percent of the egg white) there are about eleven protein molecules (11 percent). <u>Proteins</u> are large molecules that are important to living things. The protein in egg white is called <u>albumen</u>.

When egg whites are beaten, air bubbles become trapped in the egg whites. The air bubbles become trapped by the large protein molecules in the egg whites. The protein molecules trap the air bubbles by linking themselves together to form a rigid network like a fence around the air bubbles. This network of protein molecules surrounding the air bubbles is stable and can make the air bubbles last a long time. As more air becomes trapped by the protein molecules in egg whites, the volume or space taken up by the egg whites and air mixture becomes larger.

Gas trapped in a liquid is called a <u>foam</u>. At first, the trapped air bubbles are large and easy to see. However, as the egg whites are beaten longer, the larger air bubbles are broken in smaller and smaller air bubbles.

The foam becomes white when the air bubbles become smaller because the tiny air bubbles which are surrounded by protein molecules do not let light pass through the foam. The light is scattered or made to go in all directions when it strikes the foam.

Egg whites are clear before you start to beat them because the individual protein molecules are surrounded by many water molecules. When individual protein molecules are surrounded by water molecules, light passes through the mixture without being scattered very much.

Other things to try

Repeat this experiment without separating the egg (use both the egg white and yolk). Do you still form a firm, white foam when you beat the egg?

25 ARE MOLECULES IN EGG WHITE LINKED TOGETHER BY HEATING?

Materials

An egg

A stove

A pan

Two bowls

Water

A teaspoon

A measuring cup

Procedure

GET AN ADULT TO HELP YOU WITH THIS EXPERIMENT. DO NOT USE THE STOVE BY YOURSELF.

Heat a pan of water on a stove until the water begins to boil. Turn off the stove. Using a measuring cup, pour one-half cup of boiling water into a bowl. Into a second bowl pour one-half cup of cool water.

Carefully crack an egg and gently pour the clear part of the egg into a bowl. This clear liquid is called albumen or egg white. Keep the yellow yolk in the egg shell. Set the yolk aside. You only will be using the clear part of the egg.

Pour two teaspoons of clear egg white liquid into the bowl of hot water. Pour two teaspoons of clear egg white liquid into the bowl of cool water. Watch the two bowls of water.

Observations

Is the egg white or albumen a clear liquid in the egg? Does the clear liquid turn into a white, jellylike solid in either of the bowls of water? Does this clear liquid turn white in the bowl of hot water? Does this clear liquid turn white in the bowl of cool water?

EGG WHITE IN

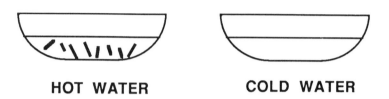

HOT WATER   **COLD WATER**

Discussion

People have been cooking and eating chicken eggs for thousands of years. It is estimated that about 400 billion eggs are eaten throughout the world every year.

The outer shell of the egg is made mostly of the mineral <u>calcium carbonate</u>. Inside the shell is the yellow yolk and the clear egg white which also is called <u>albumen</u>. The yolk is made of water, fat, and protein. The albumen is made of water and protein. The albumen is called the egg white or the white because when it is cooked it turns a white color.

<u>Protein</u> molecules are long chain molecules made of many small <u>amino acid</u> molecules linked together like beads on a string. In an unheated egg, these protein molecules are curled into many tiny balls of protein that are spread throughout the water in the white.

The energy of heating causes these protein molecules to uncoil and spread out. The higher temperature causes the motion of the protein molecules to increase. The molecules spread out as if you took a tangled string of beads and stretched it out into a long extended chain. As the molecules spread out, they attach to other stretched out proteins and link together. This process of linking proteins together is called <u>coagulation</u>.

When coagulation occurs, the proteins link together to form a white jellylike solid. When the protein molecules link together, light cannot pass through the solid. Heating causes the albumen to change from a clear liquid to a white solid. The proteins trap water molecules in this solid so it remains soft and moist. If you overheat eggs when cooking them, water is driven out and the eggs become either a dry solid or lumps of solid floating in watery liquid.

The change from separate balls of protein to linked protein molecules takes place in hot water but not in cold water. In cold water there is not enough energy to cause the molecules to unfold from tiny ball-like shapes.

In the balls of proteins, each protein molecule is linked to itself rather than to other molecules. The curled-up proteins tend to have a negative charge on the surface. Since two negative charges repel each other, the balls of protein do not come together but instead stay apart and float in the water.

Other things to try

Break open a fresh uncooked egg and a hard boiled egg. Compare their appearance and properties.

Watch as an egg is heated on a skillet, and explain the changes taking place.

26 CAN YOU SEE THE IRON IN IRON-FORTIFIED CEREALS?

Materials

Small magnet (you may have one on your refrigerator)

Plastic spoon   Facial tissue

Bowl

A package of instant fortified cereal, such as oatmeal, grits, or cream of wheat. Read the list of ingredients on the package. Use a cereal that lists reduced iron as one of the ingredients.

Procedure

Use a piece of facial tissue to clean the small magnet. This will make sure there are no iron particles on the magnet before you do this experiment.

Open a package of instant fortified cereal and pour the cereal into a bowl. Place the small magnet in the dry cereal. Use the plastic spoon to stir the magnet around the cereal. Stir for one minute. Remove the magnet and look carefully at the edges of the magnet. Rub the magnet with a piece of facial tissue.

Observations

Do you see small iron particles on the magnet after you stir the magnet in the dry fortified cereal? Can you see the iron particles on the facial tissue after you wipe the magnet with the tissue?

Discussion

Iron is found naturally in many foods, including meats, green leafy vegetables, certain beans, and whole-grain foods such as brown rice, cracked wheat, corn meal, and barley. Iron is an essential nutrient for our bodies. Iron is an important part of hemoglobin. Hemoglobin is found in blood cells and is what makes blood red in color. Hemoglobin carries oxygen from the lungs to other parts of the body.

IRON FILINGS ON
A MAGNET

Sometimes food companies add iron and other nutrients to processed foods to make the processed foods more nutritious. <u>Reduced iron</u> is one type of iron used to make some foods rich in iron. In reduced iron, the iron atoms have the same number of negative charges (electrons) and positive charges (protons). Also, the iron atoms in reduced iron are not combined with other atoms.

Sometimes food companies add <u>iron compounds</u> to processed foods to fortify the food in iron. In iron compounds, the iron atoms are combined with other types of atoms. Also, the iron atoms in iron compounds have positive charges and are called ions. Iron ions have either a +2 charge or a +3 charge. Iron with a +2 charge is called ferrous ion, and iron with a +3 charge is called ferric ion. Most iron compounds used to fortify foods in iron are ferrous compounds because the body can more easily absorb ferrous ions.

Reduced iron is added to fortified foods as very small particles called <u>iron filings</u>. You should be able to see the iron filings added to some cereals by using a magnet. Iron filings are attracted to and stick on a magnet. Iron compounds cannot be seen with a magnet because they are not attracted to a magnet like reduced iron.

Other things to try

Look on the packages of other processed foods that are fortified with iron. Is the iron reduced iron or is it combined with other atoms? Can you collect reduced iron from other foods?

27 CAN GELATIN BE USED TO DYE PLASTIC SPOONS?

Materials

Four plastic spoons

One packet of unflavored gelatin

Water

Two glasses

A two-cup Pyrex measuring cup

Vinegar

Red food coloring

Measuring spoons

Tape

A felt pen

A small saucepan

A stove

A paper towel

A large spoon

Procedure

ASK AN ADULT TO HELP YOU WITH THIS EXPERIMENT.
DO NOT USE THE STOVE BY YOURSELF.

Place a piece of tape on each spoon. Use the felt pen to label the spoons "0," "1," "2," and "3." Make sure to write on the tape.

Fill the Pyrex measuring cup with one and one-half cups of water. Add this water to a small saucepan. You will heat this water on the stove in a few minutes.

Add one-half cup of cold water to the two-cup Pyrex measuring cup. Open the packet of unflavored gelatin and pour the contents into the cold water in the two-cup measuring cup. Stir the gelatin and water with a large spoon for thirty seconds. Some of the gelatin will not dissolve in cold water.

Heat the one and one-half cups of water in the small saucepan on the stove until the water boils. Turn off the heat. Carefully pour the hot water into the two-cup measuring cup containing the gelatin solution. Stir for about one minute to dissolve the gelatin. Let the hot gelatin solution cool for fifteen minutes.

While the gelatin solution is cooling, add one teaspoon of red food coloring to one of the glasses. Add one-half cup of water to the glass. Add one-half teaspoon of vinegar to the red dye solution. Stir with a measuring spoon to mix the solution. Fill the second glass with water.

Dip the plastic spoons labeled "1," "2," and "3" in the gelatin solution for fifteen seconds. Remove the spoons and gently tap the spoons on the top of the measuring cup to remove any excess gelatin on the spoons. Place the spoons on a paper towel. Let the spoons dry for fifteen minutes.

Dip the spoons labeled "2" and "3" in the gelatin solution again for fifteen seconds. Remove the spoons and gently tap the spoons on the top of the measuring cup. Place the spoons on the paper towel to dry for fifteen minutes.

Dip the spoon labeled "3" in the gelatin solution again for fifteen seconds. Remove the spoon and gently tap the spoon on the top of the measuring cup. Place the spoon on the paper towel to dry for fifteen minutes.

Place the spoons labeled "0," "1," "2," and "3" in the red dye solution. Leave them in the red dye solution for five minutes. Remove the spoons from the red dye solution. Gently rinse them in the glass of clear water. Place the spoons on the paper towel to dry.

Observations

Can you see a layer of gelatin on the spoons labeled "1," "2," and "3?" Do all the spoons become dyed? Which spoon is the most red? Which spoon is the least red?

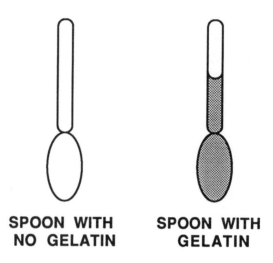

**SPOON WITH
NO GELATIN**   **SPOON WITH
GELATIN**

Discussion

Gelatin is a type of protein. Proteins are large molecules made by plants and animals. Proteins are important molecules and have many functions in living things. Gelatin is made when proteins in connective tissue of meat are cooked. Most gelatin bought in grocery stores comes from connective tissue in animal skins.

Gelatin is soluble in water. This is why the gelatin particles dissolve and disappear when you stir the gelatin in the two cups of water. When you dip the spoons in the gelatin solution, some gelatin molecules stick to the spoons. More gelatin molecules stick to the spoons each time they are dipped in the gelatin solution. The spoon labeled "3" should have the most gelatin molecules attached to it since it was dipped in the gelatin solution three times.

The spoons labeled "1," "2," and "3" should become dyed when you place them in the red dye solution. These spoons should become dyed because red food coloring molecules stick to gelatin molecules.

Red food coloring molecules are negatively charged, and gelatin molecules have many positive charges in water containing vinegar. The negatively charged red food coloring molecules form bonds with the positively charged sites on the gelatin molecules because opposite charges attract each other. The spoon labeled "3" should have the most dye on it because it has the most gelatin on it. The spoon labeled "0" should have very little red dye on it because it did not have any gelatin molecules on it.

Other things to try

Repeat the experiment using other food colorings. Do you get similar results?

Use metal spoons instead of plastic in this experiment. To remove the gelatin and dye from the metal spoons after you are finished with the experiment, use a sponge to wash them with warm water and soap.

Can you dye other solid objects?

28 CAN SUN AND AIR CAUSE VANILLA TO LOSE ITS ODOR?

Materials

A bottle of vanilla extract   A teaspoon

A small clear jar

Procedure

Pour three teaspoons of vanilla extract into a small clear jar. Close the bottle of vanilla extract. Put the closed bottle of vanilla extract in a closet or closed cabinet. Place the opened jar of vanilla extract next to a window. Choose a window that gets plenty of sunshine. Leave the jar near the window for several days.

Observations

Smell the vanilla extract that has been kept in the closed bottle. Do you smell the odor of vanilla extract? Smell the vanilla extract that was kept in the opened jar near a window. Do you smell the odor of vanilla extract?

Discussion

The vanilla extract in the bottle should have a strong odor. The vanilla extract that has been exposed to sun and air should have lost much of its odor.

Vanillin molecules are found in vanilla extract. Vanillin is a molecule made of eight carbon atoms, eight hydrogen atoms, and three oxygen atoms. Vanillin molecules give vanilla extract its odor. These molecules are found in vanilla beans that grow on the vanilla plants. Vanilla extract is used in food and beverages.

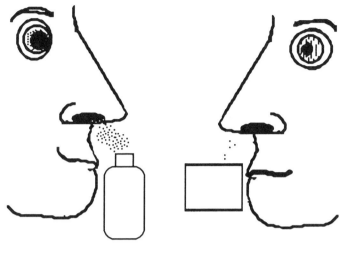

VANILLA　　**VANILLA AFTER AIR AND LIGHT EXPOSURE**

When vanillin molecules are exposed to sun and air, they can change into <u>vanillic acid</u> molecules. Vanillic acid molecules are made of eight carbon atoms, eight hydrogen atoms, and four oxygen atoms.

A vanillic acid molecule has one more oxygen atom that a vanillin molecule. Adding oxygen atoms to molecules is called <u>oxidation</u>. The oxidation changes vanillin to vanillic acid. Vanillin has a strong odor. Vanillic acid has no odor.

Air contains mostly oxygen and nitrogen molecules. Oxygen molecules in the air can combine with vanillin molecules to make vanillic acid molecules. Energy from sunlight helps cause this change to take place. The bottle of vanilla extract is kept closed so oxygen molecules from the air do not get in it.

When the vanilla extract is opened to the air, some of the water and alcohol molecules found in vanilla extract go into the air and leave the vanillin molecules in the jar. That is why there is less liquid in the jar after several days. The remaining liquid becomes thicker. At the same time, vanillin molecules are changing.

Other things to try

Repeat this experiment using various lengths of time to see how long it takes the vanilla extract to lose its odor.

Try this experiment again, but this time put the vanilla extract in a Ziploc bag and squeeze the air out of the bag to see what happens without as much oxygen from the air.

Try this experiment in the open jar, but place the jar in a dark closet to observe the effect of having less light.

Can you explain why vanilla extract always comes in dark bottles instead of clear bottles? Can you explain why you should keep bottles of vanilla extract closed?

DOES ORANGE PEEL CONTAIN A NATURAL INSECTICIDE?

29

Materials

One ant   A knife

One orange   A small jar with lid

Procedure

GET AN ADULT TO HELP YOU WITH THIS EXPERIMENT. HAVE AN ADULT CUT AND PEEL AN ORANGE. DO NOT GET THE OIL FROM THE ORANGE PEEL IN YOUR EYES. WASH YOUR HANDS AFTER DOING THIS EXPERIMENT.

It is the oil in the outer part of an orange peel that you will study in this experiment. Use a piece of orange peel about the size of your thumb. Make sure the peel is scraped clean of fruit.

Catch an ant in a jar. Squeeze the orange peel to squirt a few drops of oil from the orange peel into the jar. Cover the jar with the lid.

Watch the ant for several minutes. When you have finished with your observations, you can discard the jar.

Observations

Do you see a fine mist squirt out of the orange peel when you squeeze it? What effect does this oil have on the ant?

Discussion

An <u>insecticide</u> is a substance used to kill insects. Many artificial insecticides are used in buildings and on farms to control the number of insects. Some plants produce natural insecticides to protect themselves from insects.

Orange peel contains a natural insecticide called <u>limonene</u>. Each limonene molecule contains ten carbon atoms and sixteen hydrogen atoms. Limonene is found in many citrus fruits, including oranges, lemons, and grapefruit. Limonene helps keep insects from eating through the peel of citrus fruits. Limonene is found in the oil that is released from orange peel when the peel is squeezed.

To protect our environment, we need to understand the role of nature in our world. There is a balance in nature among different animals and plants, and we should work with this balance whenever possible. When it becomes necessary to control insects, it is better to use chemicals that do not harm the environment. Sometimes methods developed by nature to control insects may be safer than artificial means.

Other things to try

You may want to determine for yourself whether other citrus fruits contain limonene. If you squeeze a lemon or grapefruit, is a mist of oil released? Does this oil contain a natural insecticide?

CAN ELECTRICITY AND COPPER PENNIES BE USED TO DISTINGUISH CHLORIDE AND SULFATE IONS?

30

Materials

Two pieces of insulated wire (about ten inches long)

A measuring cup

A 6-volt lantern battery

Four new, shiny pennies

Epsom salt

Table salt

Two pieces of paper

Two glasses

Two teaspoons

Two paper clips

Two small plates

A pen

Water

Procedure

ASK AN ADULT TO HELP YOU WITH THIS EXPERIMENT. ELECTRICITY CAN BE DANGEROUS. <u>NEVER</u> PUT HOUSE CURRENT (electricity from a wall outlet) IN WATER. YOU SHOULD USE ONLY A SMALL BATTERY FOR THIS EXPERIMENT. DO NOT LET ANY FLAME GET NEAR YOUR EXPERIMENT.

Add four teaspoons of table salt to a glass. Add one-half cup of water to the glass. Stir for one minute to dissolve the table salt.

Carefully pour enough of the liquid from the first glass to fill a plate with table salt water. Write "table salt" on a piece of paper and place this paper beside the plate.

Add four teaspoons of Epsom salt to a second glass. Add one-half cup of water to this glass. Stir for one minute to dissolve the Epsom salt.

Carefully pour enough of the liquid from the second glass to fill a plate with Epsom salt water. Write "Epsom salt" on a piece of paper and place this paper beside the plate.

Ask an adult to remove about one-half inch of insulation from the ends of each of the wires. Attach one end of the first wire to the negative (-) terminal on the battery. Attach one end of the second wire to the positive (+) terminal on the battery. Use a paper clip across the top of each penny to attach the free end of each wire to a penny. (If you have wires with alligator clips on them you can attach the wires directly to each penny and not use paper clips.)

Hold the pennies about one-quarter inch apart and place them in the table salt water covering the first plate. Do not let the paper clips or wires touch the water. Hold the pennies in the water for about two minutes and watch the water.

If nothing happens, then you have a loose wire, bad connection, or a dead battery. Check all the wires.

Remove the pennies from the water and set them aside. Use two new pennies for the next part of the experiment. Use a paper clip across the top of each penny to attach the free end of each wire to a penny.

Hold the pennies about one-quarter inch apart and place them in the Epsom salt water covering the second plate. Do not let the paper

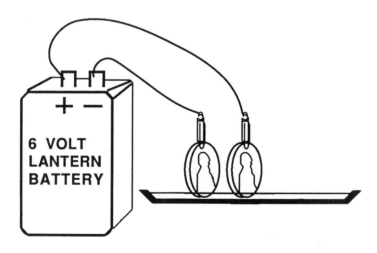

clips or wires touch the water. Hold the pennies in the water for about two minutes and watch the water.

DO NOT LET THE ELECTRICITY FLOW THROUGH THE WATER FOR MORE THAN FIVE MINUTES.

Observations

Does the water with table salt form a yellowish-green-colored solid near one of the pennies? Do you see bubbles forming around either of the pennies?

Does the water with Epsom salt form a blue-colored solid near one of the pennies? Do you see bubbles forming around either of the pennies?

Discussion

Table salt is sodium chloride. Sodium chloride is made of positive sodium atoms and negative chlorine atoms. Epsom salt is magnesium sulfate. Magnesium sulfate is made of positive magnesium atoms and negative sulfate ions. The negative sulfate ions are made of sulfur and oxygen atoms joined together.

Electrons flow into the water at the penny attached to the negative terminal (negative penny). These electrons combine with water to form hydrogen gas and hydroxide ions. A hydroxide ion is made from a hydrogen atom, an oxygen atom, and an extra electron. A substance that produces a hydroxide ion (OH-) in water is called a base. The bubbles formed at the negative penny are hydrogen gas.

At the penny attached to the positive terminal (positive penny), copper atoms leave the surface of the penny and go into the water as positive copper ions. Copper ions in water can combine with negative chlorine atoms (chloride ions) and hydroxide ions to form tiny solid particles that have a yellowish-green color. Copper ions in water can combine with negative sulfate ions and water or hydroxide to form tiny solid particles that have a blue color.

COPPER IONS ARE POISON. DO NOT PUT THE WATER IN YOUR MOUTH. POUR THE BLUE LIQUID DOWN THE DRAIN AND CLEAN THE PLATE BEFORE USING AGAIN.

Other things to try

Have a friend mix either table salt or Epsom salt in water while you are not watching. You cannot tell the difference between these two salts when dissolved in water by just looking at them. You can tell the difference by repeating the experiment above. Repeat this experiment and see if you can correctly identify the unknown salt that is dissolved in the water.

Try repeating the experiment with a mixture of both table salt (sodium chloride) and Epsom salt (magnesium sulfate) in water. What do you observe when you pass electricity through two pennies in this mixed liquid?

COMPLETE LIST OF MATERIALS USED IN THESE EXPERIMENTS

Ant

Balloons

bottle opener

bowls

bucket

Carbonated beverage in plastic bottle

carbonated beverage in glass bottle

clear dishwashing liquid

cooking oil

corn syrup

Duct tape

Egg beater

eggs

electrical tape

Epsom salt

Facial tissue

felt pen

flashlight

fluorescent light bulb

flower pots

fortified instant cereal

Garden water hose

gelatin, unflavored

glasses

gum

Hair dryer

Ice cubes

incandescent light

insulated wire

Jars with lids

Knife

Magnet

Measuring cups

measuring spoons

mercury streetlight

microwave oven

milk, lowfat (2%)

music compact disc (CD)

Newspaper

nozzle for water hose

notebook paper

Orange

Pan with lid

paper

paper clips

paper cups

paper towels

pen

pennies

plastic cups

plastic plates

plastic sandwich bags

plastic spoons

plates

popcorn

Pyrex two-cup measuring cup

Red food coloring

refrigerator freezer

rubbing alcohol

ruler

Salt

sand

saucepan

sink

6-volt lantern battery

small jars

spoons

stones

stove

sugar

Tape

teaspoons

timer

towel

Vanilla extract

vinegar

Water

INDEX